Queen Victoria

Dorothy Turner

Illustrations by Martin Salisbury

The Bookwright Press
New York · 1989

Great Lives

Beethoven
Louis Braille
Julius Caesar
Winston Churchill
Captain Cook
Marie Curie
Charles Dickens
Francis Drake
Einstein
Queen Elizabeth I
Queen Elizabeth II
Anne Frank
Gandhi
Henry VIII
Joan of Arc

Helen Keller
John F. Kennedy
Martin Luther King
John Lennon
Ferdinand Magellan
Karl Marx
Mary Queen of Scots
Mozart
Napoleon
Florence Nightingale
Elvis Presley
William Shakespeare
Tchaikovsky
Mother Teresa
Queen Victoria

First published in the United States by
The Bookwright Press
387 Park Avenue South
New York NY 10016

First published in 1988 by
Wayland (Publishers) Limited
61 Western Road, Hove
East Sussex BN3 1JD, England

© Copyright 1988 Wayland (Publishers) Ltd

Library of Congress Cataloging-in-Publication Data

Turner, Dorothy.
    Queen Victoria / by Dorothy Turner.
       p. cm. – (Great lives)
    Bibliography: p.
    Includes index.
    Summary: A biography of the nineteenth-century British monarch
whose sixty-three year reign over one-quarter of the world's
population covered a period of great industrial and social change.
    ISBN 0–531–18283–5
    1. Victoria, Queen of Great Britain, 1819–1901 – Juvenile
literature. 2. Great Britain – Kings and rulers – Biography – Juvenile
literature. 3. Great Britain – History – Victoria, 1837–1901–
–Juvenile literature. [1. Victoria, Queen of Great Britain,
1819–1901. 2. Kings, queens, rulers, etc.] I. Title. II. Series:
DA557.T87   1989
941.081′092′4–dc19
[B]
[92]   89–786
                                                    CIP
                                                    AC

Phototypeset by Kalligraphics Ltd, Horley, Surrey
Printed in Italy by G. Canale & C.S.p.A., Turin

Contents

A most perfect female child

When Princess Alexandrina Victoria was born in Kensington Palace on May 24, 1819, her parents were delighted. Her father, the Duke of Kent, at once wrote to a friend describing her as "a most perfect female child."

Her mother, the German Princess Victoria (Duchess of Kent) was also eager to share her happiness and pride. She wrote to

George III (1738–1820) was king of England when his granddaughter Victoria was born.

her own mother in Germany saying she was pleased to have a daughter because "the English like queens." Indeed the baby Victoria was in direct line to inherit the British throne.

At that time the monarchy was unpopular and in sad disarray. King George III (Victoria's grandfather) was too ill to rule competently and his seven sons were generally disliked.

George III died before Victoria was a year old. He was succeeded first by his eldest son, George IV (The Prince Regent) and then by another son, William IV, who was already sixty-five when he came to the throne. Neither of them had any surviving legitimate heirs. Although George III had had fifteen children, only one grandchild was legally able to inherit the throne – and that was Victoria.

Of course, nobody could have foreseen that she would reign longer than any other English king or queen, nor that she would make the monarchy popular again and give her name to a whole era.

The Duke and Duchess of Kent with their newborn daughter, Victoria.

A simple childhood

Victoria never knew her father, the Duke of Kent, because he died before she was a year old. For the rest of her childhood she was brought up by her mother and a much-loved German governess named Louise Lehzen.

Despite her privileged position, the young princess did not have a happy childhood. For one thing, it was lonely. Her mother knew little English, and Victoria was looked upon as a foreign "intruder" by the rest of the royal

The 13-year-old Princess Victoria was the center of attention on a visit to Brighton.

family. She was almost always with adults. Once a week a child was invited to play with her. One of these children later remembered that Victoria told her: "I may call you Jane, but you must not call me Victoria." Instead of having friends, she made and played with a huge collection of dolls.

Nor was it a life of luxury. Victoria herself wrote: "I was brought up very simply – never had a room to myself till I was nearly grown up." As a small child she attended dinner with the grown-ups, "eating my bread and milk out of a small silver basin. Tea was only allowed as a great treat in later years."

She could be hot-tempered and sometimes rather spoiled. A determination to have her own way stayed with her all her life.

Victoria's mother ensured that she had a good education. She was especially gifted in music, art and languages. But it was also a strict education, and she was not allowed to read any novels because they were thought too frivolous.

Victoria was allowed few friends, so she spent long hours playing with her dolls.

Training to be queen

Victoria was also trained for her future role as queen, being taught that a monarch "should live for others." However, it seems Victoria was not told she was to be queen until she was about eleven years old. When she was told, she said "she cried much."

Her mother insisted that Victoria should get to know the country she was to rule. For this purpose, the young princess was taken on a journey by horse-drawn carriage around the country.

It was a time of terrible contrasts in wealth and poverty, and the plight of the poor made a deep impression on Victoria. So, too, did her first glimpses of the coal mining towns of the Midlands where "the men, women, children, country and houses are all black."

These were difficult years for Victoria, as her relationship with her mother presented many problems. This was largely because the Duchess was heavily influenced by a man Victoria disliked. To pass the time, Victoria began to collect autographs. She had a fine singing voice and enjoyed going to the opera. She also read many books. Maybe she even managed to slip in a novel or two without her mother's knowledge.

Then, shortly after her eighteenth birthday, her uncle King William IV died. Early on the morning of June 20, 1837, Victoria was visited by the Archbishop of Canterbury who solemnly brought her the news. In place of an aged king, the country now had a young queen.

The young princess toured the country, seeing rich and poor alike. New industries were already changing the landscape.

What is fit and right . . .

Victoria recorded almost everything she did and thought in journals throughout her long life. She filled some 120 volumes of journals, although many were destroyed after her death, at her request. On the day she came to the throne she wrote that she would try "to fulfil my duty towards my country" and do "what is fit and right." She followed these beliefs steadfastly for the next sixty-four years.

That same day she ordered that she should – at last – have her own bedroom (she had always

Throughout her long life, Victoria kept detailed accounts of her thoughts and actions.

shared a room with her mother until then). The new queen moved to Buckingham Palace, making sure that her mother was given a set of apartments some distance from her own.

The coronation, on June 28, 1838, was hugely popular, as was the young queen. A new souvenir industry was born as pictures of Victoria appeared for sale everywhere, on books, medals and in the form of portraits.

But Victoria had a great deal to learn, and much work to do. She was instructed and guided mainly by her Prime Minister

The 18-year-old queen was crowned at Westminster on June 28, 1838.

Lord Melbourne, her "dear Lord M," who took the place of secretary as well as minister. In many ways too, he became for her the father she had never known. The queen and Melbourne met frequently and soon she was involved in all aspects of Parliament's work.

It was a heavy task for a young woman. No wonder she sometimes felt that "I do not think myself it is good fun playing queen."

Victoria and Albert

The two cousins enjoyed writing music together.

A few months after Victoria's birth, her cousin Albert was born in Germany. Already, their relations foresaw the possibility of a marriage one day between the cousins to make the family more powerful.

But no artificial match-making was required. Victoria and Albert met when they were seventeen, and she was impressed by him. The following year he visited her at Windsor. There the impression deepened. As the queen wrote: "It was with some emotion that I beheld Albert – who is *beautiful*."

Victoria proposed marriage to her eighteen-year-old cousin (as she was queen, he was not allowed to propose to her). It was, she said, "the happiest moment of my life."

Albert was never fully accepted by the English aristocracy (for whom Victoria cared very little anyway) but he had many virtues. He loved the arts, was intelligent and was deeply

devoted to his wife. He also came to play an increasing part in British government.

On February 10, 1840, the couple were married, both age twenty. A splendid ceremony was followed by a lavish reception at Buckingham Palace, with a wedding cake almost 3 meters (10ft) wide, decorated with cupids and doves.

It was a time of great happiness, and that happiness lasted for the next twenty-one years. Victoria followed this with forty years of devoted widowhood. The marriage of Victoria and Albert was to be one of the most famous in history.

Albert and Victoria at their wedding. It was a happy occasion.

A growing family

Within a year of their marriage, Victoria gave birth to the first of their children. When the doctor told her the baby was a girl, Victoria said "Never mind, the next one will be a Prince." The child was called Victoria, known in the family as Vicky.

A year later the predicted son was born. He was christened Albert, but was known as Bertie.

Victoria and Albert had nine children, each in quick succession. Later, writing to her daughter

The young couple's family grew rapidly.

Vicky, the queen explained that she had found these many pregnancies a great irritation and a burden on her health.

Victoria continued to be busy with overseeing the work of her ministers and Parliament. Albert, too, played an active and increasingly important part in this work. He reorganized the royal household more efficiently and economically. But he had Victoria's governess, Louise Lehzen, sent back to Germany. Only he would supervise the upbringing of the royal children. Victoria was very sad to lose her.

That Christmas of 1841, Albert wrote with pride of his children and their "happy wonder at the German Christmas tree and its radiant candles" – a fashion then new to England and one which Albert helped to make popular.

Although they were both tireless workers, Albert and Victoria also made time to enjoy their children.

Houses in the country

Victoria and Albert enjoyed nothing better than taking their family away into the fresh air for vacations, for they both disliked London.

In 1842 the family made their first visit to Scotland. The queen fell in love with the Highlands and its people. It was a love affair that lasted all her life. Later she had Balmoral rebuilt as a royal Scottish vacation home, which it still is today.

Another favorite place was the Isle of Wight. There they rebuilt Osborne House as a vacation hideway. Osborne provided the family with welcome privacy. The children had a fort and a play cottage in the garden. Years later, Victoria was even able to try out a tricycle behind the secrecy of its walls. (She enjoyed the exciting experience!) She also enjoyed horse-back riding, especially as it made her seem taller than her actual short height.

As railroads spread across Britain, travel became easier for everyone. The Industrial Revolution was changing the country and the lives of its people. In 1851, Victoria visited the north of England and noticed how the factory workers of Manchester were "painfully unhealthy looking."

In the same year, the advances made by industry and technology were celebrated at the Great Exhibition. This was held in Hyde Park, London in the specially built Crystal Palace, a wonder of glass and steel.

Victoria opened the exhibition with great pride, for her beloved Albert had played an active part in setting it up.

The Great Exhibition of 1851 was a showcase for British industry.

The queen especially enjoyed riding at Balmoral, in Scotland.

Death in life

The Crimean War (1854–56) was the only European war that Britain was involved in during the whole of Victoria's long reign. During this war, troops were sent to fight Russia on the Crimean Peninsula.

It was there that Florence Nightingale became a national heroine, when she took over the running of the army hospitals. On her return to England she and Victoria met each other on several occasions. These two strong and determined woman had much in common and always got on splendidly with each other.

Florence Nightingale tending the wounded soldiers during the Crimean War. She and Victoria greatly admired each other.

Meanwhile, Albert and Victoria continued to work hard, with Albert becoming increasingly involved in helping the poor. He was particularly interested in plans for introducing better housing, and he put his ideas into practice on the various royal estates.

By the time they were both thirty-nine years old they were also grandparents, for their eldest daughter Vicky had married Prince Frederick William, heir to the Prussian throne, and produced a son.

But Victoria now faced the darkest time of her life. In March 1861 her mother died. Within ten months, Albert, too, had died, a victim of typhoid fever. He was only forty-two.

The nation went into shocked mourning. Victoria was, of course, devastated. "I may drag on an utterly extinguished life," she wrote to her daughter, "but it will be death in life."

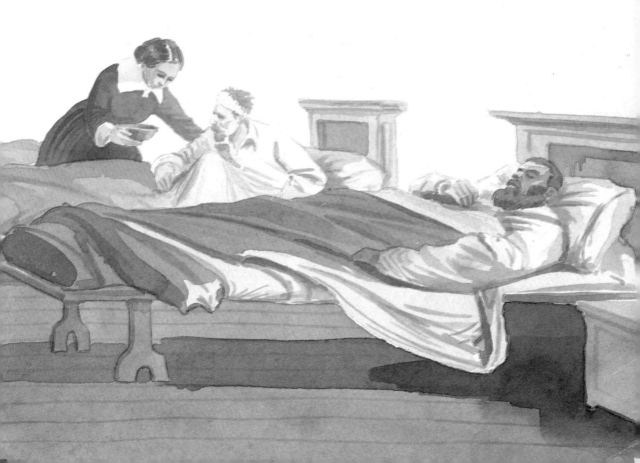

A changing monarchy

During the next forty years Victoria made only a few public appearances, and she wore black for every day of those years except one. She made no more outings to the theater or opera. She ordered Albert's room to be left exactly as it had been before his death.

The queen set about erecting monuments to Albert. One of his favorite projects was also made a reality: the building of an arts and science center in London. Today we owe the Albert Hall, the Natural History Museum and the Victoria and Albert Museum to Albert's ideas.

Above *The Natural History Museum in London.*

Below *The Albert Hall, a circular concert hall dedicated to Albert.*

Many people at first found this devotion to her late husband excessive; however Victoria did gradually begin to recover. She published a selection from some of her journals, describing her life with Albert on their visits to Scotland. Her book was a huge success, and brought her great popularity. As a commentator wrote at the time, it made the royal family appear "in a new and more human light." This is a tradition that Britain's modern royal family has continued, with its willingness to appear on television and in movies.

Another way in which Victoria strengthened the monarchy was

by breaking its traditional allegiance to a particular political party. Albert had convinced her of the wisdom of not taking sides. She listened to all her Prime Ministers, favored some above others, made her opinions known to them, but did not insist on their agreeing with her. Of her ministers, she particularly liked Benjamin Disraeli, who was a Tory. However, she claimed that William Gladstone, (the leader of the Liberal Party and her Prime Minister four times) tired her out and she generally disliked him.

Left *The Albert Memorial, London.*

Below *Benjamin Disraeli, a favorite Prime Minister.*

Queen and Empress

The Victorian Age – for so it came to be called – was a long era of peace and prosperity for Britain. Victory overseas had brought new territories. Trade flourished. When in 1875 Britain gained control of the Suez Canal, the route through Egypt connecting the Mediterranean and Red Seas, the journey to British India was made much quicker. The following year Victoria added Empress of India to her titles.

She continued to work tirelessly. Various near-disasters and tragedies befell her. In all, she survived six assassination

The Suez Canal played an important part in the spread of the British Empire.

attempts. Illness claimed many of those who were dearest to her, including her daughter Alice. Alice died on December 14, 1878, seventeen years to the day since the death of Albert. "This terrible day come round again," recorded the queen in her journal. The following year her son Leopold died. As there were then so many illnesses that were not curable, it is scarcely surprising that the Victorians were often in mourning.

Despite these tragedies, the queen continued to rule her household strictly. Her desire to have her own way at all times made her a formidable character. For example, she insisted every evening after dinner that all her guests should stand in her presence until it was time to go to bed at 11 pm. Nobody could speak to her unless she invited them to do so. Anyone who tried to lean against something for support was sharply reprimanded. She, of course, could sit.

When theater groups or musicians came to entertain her, nobody was allowed to applaud or laugh until the queen had done so first. Yet she was not always stern. She enjoyed laughing and was even known to dance on occasion.

The queen could be a formidable character, demanding high standards of behavior from all those around her.

What an Empire! What a Queen!

In 1887 Victoria had reigned for fifty years. To mark this Golden Jubilee, a ceremony was held at Westminster Abbey. The queen made one of her rare public appearances in a huge procession that included kings, queens, princes and princesses from all over the world. Not least among them were the queen's own family, which with her many European relatives made an impressive gathering.

Ten years later, Victoria celebrated sixty years on the throne. No previous British monarch had ruled so long, and a new name had to be invented for this occasion: a Diamond Jubilee.

This time the festivities celebrated the might of the British Empire. By now the queen's health was failing (she was seventy-eight years old) and she could not walk well. Her sight was also poor. The

Victoria at the Golden Jubilee celebrations, one of her rare public appearances after the death of Albert.

A map of the world in 1886, showing the extent of the British Empire (colored red).

procession through the streets of London was followed by a short service outside Saint Paul's Cathedral. For the first and only time since Albert's death, Victoria came out of mourning and wore a white and gold dress.

The power of the Empire was there for all to see in the procession. Soldiers and citizens from Australia, Canada, South Africa, New Zealand, Rhodesia (now Zimbabwe) and India marched together. All these countries were British red on the world map.

As part of the celebrations, Victoria sent an electric telegraph message which was relayed across the globe to her subjects.

The last years

The telegraph was just one of many inventions that were changing Britain. Victoria had ruled so long that a new world was appearing around her, and it was not always to her taste. She disliked telephones and continued to send written messages. She also disapproved of motor cars and had them banned from Hyde Park.

To the end, she continued to work extremely hard and conscientiously. When in 1899 the Boer War broke out in South Africa between British and Dutch settlers, Victoria telegraphed messages to her generals and followed their progress on large maps. But she hated war, just as she disliked the business of politics. As she wrote when younger: "I love peace and quiet – in fact I hate politics and turmoil."

In her own words the Queen was now a "portly elderly lady." No doubt she was kept portly by the enormous amounts of food it was said she enjoyed.

It became clear, however, that Victoria was ailing. She retired to Osborne House on the Isle of Wight. Only then, in the days before her death, did she allow her youngest and closest daughter Beatrice to see her in bed for the first time since childhood. There she died on January 22, 1901, aged eighty-one.

She was buried at Windsor, beside Albert in a special

Left *The queen retired to her home on the Isle of Wight as her health began to fail.*

mausoleum. Her eldest son, Bertie, came to the throne as King Edward VII. It was the beginning of a new century and the end of an age.

Queen Victoria's funeral procession at Windsor. She was deeply and sincerely mourned by her people.

The Victorian Age

Britain saw incredible changes during Victoria's long reign. The prosperity of the age led to great optimism, as well as some improvement in the plight of the poor. Many of the things we take for granted today, such as telephones, cars, trains, trade unions, gas, electricity and clean water supplies, were first introduced during her reign.

In the midst of all this change, Victoria managed to keep the monarchy steady and even gave

Some of the changes that took place during Victoria's reign.

it a new popularity. All this was at a time when other European royal families were being overthrown by revolution and war. One reason she was able to achieve this was that she was herself popular. She brought back respectability to the royal family. She also stood back to let government be ruled by Parliament. Democracy was increased, while the monarchy became the focus for general public affection.

Important, too, was her apparent ordinariness and simplicity. She was no remote aristocrat but a lively, energetic woman. She took her role as queen seriously and carried it out with great dignity, but she was also obviously a human being like her subjects. As one of her Prime Ministers, Lord Salisbury, said, "She had an extraordinary knowledge of what her people would think." In the words of a French newspaper article, published at her death: "Victoria was more than a queen, being, as it were, the head of all English families."

Right *Victoria brought a new dignity and strength to the monarchy.*

Important dates

1819   Princess Alexandrina Victoria born.

1820   Death of George III. Accession of George IV. Death of her father, the Duke of Kent.

1830   Death of George IV. William IV comes to the throne.

1837   Death of William IV. Victoria comes to the throne.

1840   Victoria and Albert marry (February). First child, Victoria, born (November).

1841   Second child, Albert, born.

1842   First visit to Scotland.

1851   The Great Exhibition.

1854–6   The Crimean War.

1861   Victoria's mother dies. Albert dies (December 14).

1870   Franco-Prussian war. French empire overthrown.

1875   British gain Suez Canal.

1876   Victoria declared Empress of India.

1887   The Golden Jubilee (50 years).

1897   The Diamond Jubilee (60 years).

1899   Boer War breaks out between British and Dutch settlers in South Africa.

1901   Victoria dies (22 January). The Prince of Wales, Albert (Bertie) comes to the throne as King Edward VII.

Glossary

Allegiance   Loyalty.

Aristocracy   The class of nobles.

Boer   A South African settler of Dutch origin.

Coronation   The ceremony of crowning a king or queen.

Democracy   System of government in which the power is in the hands of the people.

Diamond Jubilee   Celebration of a sixtieth anniversary, jubilee meaning "joyous occasion."

Empire   A widespread group of states or countries all ruled by the same monarch or leader.

Golden Jubilee   Celebration of a fiftieth anniversary.

Heir   A person next in line to inherit a title, or the throne of a country.

Industrial Revolution   The growth of industry in Britain in the nineteenth century, brought about by the development of machinery.

Legitimate   Legal; born to parents legally married to each other.

Liberal Party   This party first became known as the Liberal Party under Gladstone. Formerly the Whigs. The party stood for democratic freedom and social reform.

Mausoleum   A magnificent tomb in which famous people are buried.

Monarch   A king or queen who inherits the title from the previous king or queen.

Monarchy   A system of government headed by a king or queen.

Optimism   A favorable and hopeful view of events.

Prussia   A state in northern central Europe, now part of Germany.

Regent   Person appointed to rule a kingdom in the place of the monarch, either because the monarch is too young, absent or incapable of ruling.

Souvenir   Object that helps to recall the past or a special occasion.

Suez Canal   A canal, opened in 1869, linking the Mediterranean with the Red Sea. It saved ships the long journey around Africa to reach India.

Tory   A member of the Conservative Party.

Typhoid   A severe, sometimes fatal, fever spread in infected food and water. It was quite common in Victoria's time but is rare today.

Books to read

David Copperfield by Charles Dickens. Houghton Mifflin, 1958

Charles Dickens by Nigel Hunger. Bookwright, 1989

Finding out about Victorian London by Michael Rawcliffe. David & Charles, 1983

For Queen & Country: Victorian England by Margaret Drabble. Houghton Mifflin, 1979

Life in Victorian London by L. C. Seaman. David & Charles, 1973

Living Through History: Victorian London by Richard Tames. David & Charles, 1984

Picture acknowledgments
BBC Hulton 14; Mary Evans 4, 6, 12; Fotomas Index 22; The Mansell Collection 16, 25; Topham Picture Library title page, 27; Wayland Picture Library 21.

Index